UNLEASH YOUR POTENTIAL:

A Guide to Achieving Productivity and Success in 2023

MAXWELL FORGE

Thanks to God for the ability to write this book and those who purchased this book hoping for a better life,may you find answers,solutions and all you need to achieve success in your endeavors in this book.

CONTENTS

Chapter 1
Chapter 2
Chapter 3
Chapter 4
Chapter 5
Chapter 6
Chapter 7
Chapter 8
Chapter 9
Chapter 10
Conclusion

INTRODUCTION

Setting the Stage for Success

Welcome to "Unleash Your Potential: A Guide to Achieving Productivity and Success in 2023." As we stand on the threshold of the remaining part of the year, this is your opportunity to seize the reins of your life and transform your aspirations into accomplishments. In this introductory chapter, we'll illuminate the path ahead and delve into the key elements that will propel you towards productivity and success.

Embracing the Growth Mindset: The journey you're about to embark upon is grounded in the concept of a growth mindset. It's the belief that your abilities and intelligence can be developed through dedication, effort, and learning. As we explore the strategies within this book, remember that your potential is not fixed; it's a canvas waiting for you to paint upon with the colors of determination and continuous improvement.

The Power of Goal Setting: The pages ahead are designed to guide you in setting powerful and achievable goals for the remainder of 2023. Goals are like guiding stars—they provide direction and purpose to your efforts. By setting specific, measurable, achievable, relevant, and time-bound (SMART) goals, you're not just dreaming; you're crafting a roadmap to success.

A Glimpse into the Chapters: Throughout this book, you'll find insights, techniques, and exercises that have the potential to transform your daily life. From mastering time management and enhancing your focus to overcoming procrastination and building resilient habits, each chapter is a stepping stone towards unlocking your potential.

Your Personal Journey: The journey you're about to undertake is unique to you. It's not about mirroring someone else's success, but about discovering your own path. Each chapter will provide you with practical tools and insights, but it's up to you to tailor them to fit your circumstances and aspirations.

As you turn the pages and dive into the chapters that follow, remember that success is not just a destination—it's a journey. It's about progress, growth, and the choices you make every day. You have the power to shape your future, to mold it into something extraordinary.

So, let's embark on this journey together. Let's set the stage for success in the remaining part of 2023 and beyond. The canvas is blank, and the possibilities are endless. Get ready to unleash your potential, redefine your limits, and create a life that resonates with purpose and achievement.

Chapter 1

Mastering Time Management

Time, the most precious and finite resource, is the currency of productivity and success. In this chapter, we embark on a journey to master the art of time management—a skill that will serve as the foundation for your accomplishments in the remaining part of 2023.

Evaluating Your Current Habits:Before we dive into the strategies for effective time management, take a moment to evaluate your current habits. Reflect on how you allocate your time each day. Are there patterns of procrastination, distractions, or tasks that consume more time than they should? Identifying these habits is the first step towards transformation.

Prioritization the Key to Productivity: Imagine your time as a limited budget, and tasks as expenses. To maximize your "budget," you must prioritize tasks based on their importance and urgency. Learn the Eisenhower Matrix—quadrants that categorize tasks as urgent/important, important/not urgent, urgent/not important, and neither urgent nor important. This tool helps you allocate your time wisely, focusing on tasks that align with your goals.

The Pomodoro Technique: Have you ever felt overwhelmed by a seemingly insurmountable task? The Pomodoro Technique is your ally. This time management method involves breaking work into focused intervals (usually 25 minutes) followed by a short break. Each interval is a "Pomodoro." This technique enhances focus and combats burnout, making even the most daunting tasks manageable.

Eliminating Time-Wasters: Distractions lurk everywhere, ready to steal your time. Identify your biggest time-wasters—social media, excessive email checking, or random internet browsing—and implement strategies to minimize them. Use website blockers, designate specific times for checking emails, or employ the "two-minute rule" for quick tasks. Reclaim your time from these stealthy thieves.

Creating a Time-Blocking Schedule: Enter the world of time blocking—a method that involves scheduling specific blocks of time for different tasks. Allocate time for focused work, breaks, and personal activities. This not only keeps you on track but also prevents burnout and ensures a balanced routine.

Technology as a Time Management Tool: Technology, when used mindfully, can be your ally in time management. Explore productivity apps that assist in task organization, reminders, and goal tracking. Leverage digital calendars to plan your days effectively and stay organized.

Reflecting and Adapting: Time management is not a static process—it's an evolving journey. Regularly review your schedule, tasks, and goals. Are you making progress? Are there adjustments needed? Embrace the flexibility to adapt and refine your time management strategies based on your experiences.

As you navigate the landscape of time management, remember that mastery doesn't happen overnight. It's a skill that grows with practice and persistence. By employing the techniques in this chapter, you're not just managing minutes; you're harnessing the power to shape your days, achieve your goals, and create a life that's balanced, productive, and deeply satisfying. Embrace the art of mastering time, and watch as your journey towards success gains momentum.

Chapter 2

Goal Setting for Success

Goals are the compass that guides us towards our desired destinations. In this chapter, we delve into the art of goal setting—an essential skill that will propel you towards success in the remaining part of 2023.

Setting SMART Goals: The foundation of effective goal setting lies in crafting SMART goals—Specific, Measurable, Achievable, Relevant, and Time-bound. These goals are not mere wishes; they are the blueprints that transform dreams into actionable plans.

Breaking Down Large Goals: Ambitious goals can be overwhelming. Break them down into smaller, manageable steps. This approach not only makes the journey less daunting but also allows you to celebrate incremental victories along the way.

Tracking Progress: Without tracking, goals are like ships lost at sea. Create a system to monitor your progress. Visual tools like charts, journals, or digital trackers provide insights into your journey, helping you stay on course.

Flexibility and Adaptation: Life is dynamic, and so are your goals. Embrace the concept of adaptive goal setting. As circumstances change, be willing to adjust your goals while keeping your ultimate vision intact.

The Power of Visualization: Visualization is a powerful tool to manifest your goals. Create a mental image of your success. Imagine the emotions, sights, and sounds associated with achieving your goals. This technique not only motivates but also fuels your determination.

Accountability and Support: Share your goals with someone you trust—a friend, mentor, or coach. Accountability provides an external push, and sharing your journey with a supportive individual adds a layer of encouragement.

Mindset Matters: Cultivate a growth mindset when setting goals. Embrace challenges and setbacks as part of the journey. Approach failures as opportunities to learn and refine your approach.

In this chapter, you're not just setting goals; you're igniting a transformation. You're sculpting a future that aligns with your aspirations. As you craft each goal with intention and purpose, remember that success is not a destination; it's a continuous journey of growth and self-discovery. Armed with SMART goals, you're equipped to move forward with clarity, determination, and the unwavering belief that you're capable of achieving greatness.

Chapter 3

Cultivating Effective Habits

Habits, those quiet architects of our lives, shape our days and define our success. In this chapter, we embark on a transformative journey to understand the science of habit formation and learn how to cultivate effective habits that will propel you toward success in the remaining part of 2023.

The Power of Habits: Habits are the building blocks of our routines. They operate on autopilot, conserving mental energy while driving our actions. Understanding the cues, routines, and rewards that form habits is key to leveraging them for positive change.

Identifying Unproductive Habits: Take stock of your daily habits. Are they propelling you forward or holding you back? Identify habits that drain your time and energy, hindering your progress.

The Habit Loop: Habits follow a loop: cue, routine, reward. By identifying cues triggering unproductive habits, you can replace routines with positive actions that yield the same rewards.

The 21/90 Rule: Experts say it takes 21 days to form a habit and 90 days to solidify it. Embrace this rule as you cultivate new habits. Consistency is your ally, transforming actions from intentional efforts to ingrained behaviors.

Keystone Habits: Certain habits act as catalysts, triggering a chain reaction of positive change. These keystone habits—like exercise or daily reflection—have a ripple effect, influencing other aspects of your life.

Habit Stacking: Incorporate new habits by "stacking" them onto existing routines. This technique capitalizes on habits you already have, making it easier to introduce new ones.

Mindful Repetition: Repetition is the mother of skill. Practice and consistency are vital to habit formation. Mindfully repeat desired actions, ensuring they become second nature.

Rewarding Progress: Celebrate small victories along your habit journey. Rewards reinforce positive behavior and make the process enjoyable.

Overcoming Setbacks: Habits are not immune to setbacks. If you stumble, don't despair. Instead, view setbacks as opportunities to learn and refine your approach.

In this chapter, you're not just adopting habits; you're crafting a lifestyle that aligns with your aspirations. By replacing unproductive habits with effective ones, you're rewriting the script of your daily existence. Remember, every action you take is a vote for the person you wish to become. Embrace the power of cultivating effective habits, and watch as your life transforms, one intentional action at a time.

Chapter 4

Enhancing Focus and Concentration

In a world brimming with distractions, the ability to focus is a superpower. In this chapter, we embark on a journey to enhance your focus and concentration—a skill that will be your compass to navigate the sea of tasks and achieve success in the remaining part of 2023.

The Battle Against Distractions: Distractions are stealthy invaders, stealing precious minutes from your day. Identify common distractions—social media, notifications, clutter—and take proactive steps to mitigate their impact.

Mindfulness: The Focus Anchor: Mindfulness, the practice of being fully present in the moment, is your ally in regaining focus. Engage in mindful activities like deep breathing or meditation to cultivate concentration.

Single-Tasking vs. Multitasking: Contrary to popular belief, multitasking hampers productivity. Embrace single-tasking—focusing on one task at a time. This approach not only improves concentration but also results in higher-quality work.

The Power of Deep Work: Deep work, a state of flow where you're completely immersed in a task, leads to remarkable productivity. Allocate dedicated blocks of time for deep work, free from distractions and interruptions.

Creating a Distraction-Free Environment: Design your workspace for optimal focus. Clear clutter, organize your tools, and establish a serene atmosphere that fosters concentration.

Time Blocking for Focused Work: Employ the technique of time blocking to allocate specific chunks of time to focused work. During these periods, eliminate interruptions and immerse yourself in your tasks.

Digital Detox and Notifications Management: Take control of your digital life. Schedule periods for a digital detox, disconnecting from screens to recharge your focus. Manage notifications to prevent interruptions.

Rest and Breaks for Renewed Focus: Fatigue erodes focus. Prioritize rest and breaks to recharge your mental faculties. The Pomodoro Technique (working for focused intervals followed by short breaks) can be invaluable.

Overcoming Mental Clutter: Mental clutter—ruminating thoughts, worries—can fracture your focus. Engage in mindfulness practices, journaling, or visualization to declutter your mind and sharpen your focus.

Practice Makes Perfect: Enhancing focus is akin to building a muscle. Consistent practice leads to improvement. Gradually extend your focused periods, embracing challenges that bolster your concentration.

In this chapter, you're not just enhancing focus; you're cultivating a mindset that honors deep, meaningful work. By navigating distractions and immersing yourself in focused tasks, you're sowing the seeds of success. Remember, your attention is a precious resource—invest it wisely, and watch as your productivity, accomplishments, and sense of fulfillment soar to new heights.

Chapter 5

Boosting Energy and Well-being

Vitality is the cornerstone of productivity and success. In this chapter, we embark on a transformative journey to enhance your energy levels and well-being—a journey that will empower you to conquer the challenges of the remaining part of 2023 with vigor and vitality.

Understanding the Energy Equation: Energy is a limited resource, and how you manage it directly impacts your productivity. Explore the concepts of physical, mental, and emotional energy and learn how to optimize each.

Prioritizing Sleep: Sleep, the ultimate energy restorer, is often underestimated. Prioritize sleep by establishing a consistent sleep schedule, creating a sleep-conducive environment, and practicing relaxation techniques.

Nutrition for Sustained Energy: Your diet plays a pivotal role in energy levels. Embrace balanced meals rich in whole grains, lean proteins, fruits, and vegetables. Stay hydrated and avoid energy-draining processed foods.

Physical Activity for Vitality: Regular exercise is a potent energy booster. Find a form of exercise you enjoy and incorporate it into your routine. It enhances mood, reduces stress, and increases overall energy.

Stress Management and Mindfulness: Unmanaged stress saps your energy. Adopt stress management techniques such as deep breathing, meditation, and mindfulness. These practices rejuvenate your mental reserves.

Digital Detox for Mental Renewal: Digital devices consume considerable mental energy. Implement regular digital detox periods to recharge your mind. Engage in activities that inspire creativity and mental clarity.

Emotional Well-being: Emotional well-being is a cornerstone of energy. Cultivate positive emotions through activities you love, spend time with loved ones, and seek professional support when needed.

Balancing Work and Rest: A relentless work pace depletes energy. Embrace the importance of breaks and rest. Incorporate the 50/10 rule (50 minutes of focused work followed by a 10-minute break) for optimal productivity.

The Power of Laughter and Joy: Laughter is a natural energy booster. Engage in activities that bring you joy, surround yourself with positivity, and find humor in everyday life.

Personal Care and Self-Care Rituals: Personal care rituals rejuvenate your body and mind. Incorporate practices like skincare routines, baths, or hobbies that provide a sense of accomplishment and relaxation.

In this chapter, you're not just boosting energy; you're nurturing the wellspring of your vitality. By prioritizing sleep, nourishing your body, and managing stress, you're crafting a foundation of resilience. Embrace these practices, and watch as your energy becomes a force that propels you toward success, even in the face of challenges. Remember, you are your most valuable asset—invest in your well-being, and reap the dividends of a vibrant and thriving life.

Chapter 6

Maximizing Work Efficiency

Efficiency is the cornerstone of productivity. In this chapter, we embark on a transformative journey to enhance your work efficiency—a journey that will empower you to accomplish more and achieve success in the remaining part of 2023.

Streamlining Work Processes: Efficiency begins with streamlined processes. Assess your workflows and identify bottlenecks. Simplify complex tasks, eliminate redundancies, and create efficient sequences of actions.

Technology as a Tool: Leverage technology to automate and optimize tasks. Utilize productivity apps, task management software, and communication tools to streamline collaboration and information sharing.

Effective Task Management: Embrace effective task management techniques. Prioritize tasks using methods like the Eisenhower Matrix or ABCD prioritization. This ensures you tackle high-impact tasks first.

Batching Similar Tasks: Batching involves grouping similar tasks and completing them in a single dedicated time block. This minimizes task-switching and enhances focus, increasing overall efficiency.

Delegate and Outsource: Recognize that you can't do everything alone. Delegate tasks that can be handled by others and consider outsourcing non-core activities to free up your time.

Efficient Communication: Communication is a cornerstone of efficiency. Use concise and clear communication methods. Embrace tools like email templates and standardized communication practices.

Effective Meetings: Meetings can be time drains if not managed efficiently. Set clear objectives, distribute agendas beforehand, and limit meeting durations. Ensure meetings are productive and actionable.

Time Management Techniques: Explore various time management techniques such as the 2-Minute Rule, Time Blocking, and the Pomodoro Technique. Tailor these methods to suit your workflow and preferences.

Continuous Learning: Invest time in continuous learning. Acquiring new skills and knowledge enhances your efficiency. Stay up-to-date with industry trends and new tools that can streamline your work.

Feedback and Reflection: Regularly reflect on your work processes and seek feedback from colleagues or mentors. Continuous improvement is the hallmark of an efficient professional.

In this chapter, you're not just maximizing work efficiency; you're engineering a more productive version of yourself. By optimizing workflows, embracing technology, and refining communication, you're sculpting a path that leads to higher output and accomplishment. Remember, efficiency is the bridge between effort and results—cross it with purpose and determination, and watch as your productivity skyrockets, propelling you towards the pinnacle of success.

Chapter 7

Overcoming Procrastination

Procrastination, the silent thief of time, robs us of our potential. In this chapter, we embark on a transformative journey to overcome procrastination—a journey that will empower you to seize control of your time and achieve success in the remaining part of 2023.

Understanding Procrastination: Procrastination often stems from a desire to avoid discomfort or uncertainty. Recognize the patterns of procrastination in your life and the triggers that lead to delays.

The Two-Minute Rule: Simple tasks can often be completed in two minutes or less. Embrace the two-minute rule—when a task arises, if it can be done in two minutes, do it immediately. This minimizes tasks piling up.

Breaking Tasks into Smaller Steps: Overwhelming tasks breed procrastination. Break down tasks into smaller, manageable steps. Completing these steps creates a sense of progress and reduces the urge to delay.

Time-Boxing and Deadline Setting: Set specific time limits for tasks using time-boxing. Knowing there's a set time for a task increases focus and minimizes the temptation to procrastinate.

The 5-Second Rule: When the impulse to procrastinate strikes, countdown from five and take action. This technique interrupts the cycle of hesitation and compels you to begin tasks promptly.

Visualizing the End Result: Visualize the satisfaction and relief of completing a task. This mental image counteracts the discomfort associated with starting and encourages immediate action.

Creating a Procrastination-Free Environment: Design your environment to minimize distractions and triggers for procrastination. Set up a designated workspace that fosters focus and minimizes the temptation to delay.

Embracing the Growth Mindset: Adopt a growth mindset toward tasks that trigger procrastination. Approach challenges as opportunities for growth rather than obstacles to avoid.

Rewarding Progress: Celebrate small victories along the way. Reward yourself after completing tasks to reinforce the behavior of overcoming procrastination.

Accountability and Support: Share your goals and progress with an accountability partner. Their encouragement and support can deter procrastination and keep you on track.

In this chapter, you're not just overcoming procrastination; you're reclaiming ownership of your time. By breaking the chains of delay and embracing proactive action, you're paving a path to achievement and success. Remember, every moment spent overcoming procrastination is an investment in a more purposeful and fulfilling life. Embrace the strategies within, and watch as your days transform from a battleground of delays into a canvas of accomplishments.

ation part of 2023.

Chapter 8

Navigating Challenges and Resilience

Life's journey is marked by challenges, but your ability to navigate them with resilience determines your trajectory towards success. In this chapter, we delve into the art of overcoming challenges and cultivating resilience—a skill set that will empower you to triumph over adversity in the remaining part of 2023.

Understanding Challenges: Challenges are not roadblocks; they're opportunities for growth. Shift your perspective from seeing challenges as obstacles to viewing them as stepping stones toward personal and professional development.

Embracing Resilience: Resilience is the capacity to bounce back from setbacks. Understand that setbacks are a natural part of any journey. Embrace a resilient mindset that views challenges as temporary and surmountable.

Growth Through Adversity: Challenges cultivate strength and wisdom. Reflect on past challenges you've overcome and the growth that resulted from them. This reflection fuels your confidence in facing current and future challenges.

Adapting to Change: Change is constant, and adaptability is a hallmark of resilience. Embrace change as an opportunity to learn, grow, and evolve. Flexibility in the face of change enables you to thrive.

Positive Self-Talk: Your inner dialogue shapes your response to challenges. Replace self-doubt with positive affirmations and self-encouragement. This shift in self-talk strengthens your resolve to tackle challenges.

Developing Coping Strategies: Equip yourself with coping strategies that promote resilience. Practice deep breathing, mindfulness, or engaging in hobbies to manage stress and anxiety during challenging times.

Seeking Support: You don't have to face challenges alone. Seek support from friends, family, mentors, or professionals. Sharing your challenges lessens their weight and opens doors to solutions.

Learning from Setbacks: Rather than dwelling on setbacks, dissect them for lessons. What can you learn from the experience? How can you apply this knowledge to avoid similar pitfalls in the future?

Staying Solution-Focused: When faced with challenges, focus on solutions rather than dwelling on problems. Brainstorm creative approaches, leverage your resources, and take calculated risks to overcome hurdles.

Building a Resilience Toolkit: Create a toolkit of strategies that foster resilience. Incorporate activities that nourish your mental, emotional, and physical well-being, such as exercise, meditation, journaling, and spending time in nature.

In this chapter, you're not just navigating challenges; you're forging a resilient spirit that stands unwavering in the face of adversity. By embracing setbacks as opportunities for growth, you're building a foundation of strength and tenacity. Remember, challenges are not roadblocks but crossroads—points of decision where you can choose to rise above. Embrace the strategies within this chapter, and watch as challenges become the catalysts that propel you toward greater heights of success and personal fulfillment.

Chapter 9

Building Meaningful Relationships

Relationships are the cornerstone of a fulfilled and successful life. In this chapter, we embark on a transformative journey to understand the power of building meaningful relationships—a journey that will enrich your personal and professional life in the remaining part of 2023.

The Role of Relationships: Relationships provide support, inspiration, and a sense of belonging. Understand that investing in relationships is an investment in your well-being and success.

Networking with Purpose: Networking goes beyond collecting business cards. Approach networking with authenticity, seeking to build genuine connections rather than transactional relationships.

Cultivating Empathy: Empathy is the bedrock of meaningful relationships. Put yourself in others' shoes, listen actively, and understand their perspectives. Empathy fosters connection and trust.

Effective Communication: Communication is the bridge to understanding. Hone your communication skills—both verbal and nonverbal—to express your thoughts clearly and connect with others on a deeper level.

Nurturing Existing Relationships: Don't underestimate the value of nurturing existing relationships. Regularly check in, show appreciation, and invest time in maintaining the connections that matter to you.

Balancing Giving and Receiving: Meaningful relationships are a two-way street. Contribute to others' well-being through your actions, but also allow yourself to receive support when needed.

Boundaries for Healthy Relationships: Set clear boundaries that define your comfort zones. Healthy relationships thrive when both parties respect each other's boundaries.

Conflict Resolution: Conflicts are inevitable, but how you navigate them determines the health of your relationships. Approach conflicts with an open mind, active listening, and a willingness to find common ground.

Supportive Community: Surround yourself with people who uplift and support you. Cultivate a community that encourages your growth and provides a safe space to share your aspirations.

Mentorship and Role Models: Seek out mentors and role models who inspire you. Their guidance and insights can offer invaluable perspectives as you navigate your personal and professional journey.

In this chapter, you're not just building relationships; you're nurturing connections that add depth and meaning to your life. By investing in genuine interactions, active listening, and cultivating a supportive community, you're crafting a network that bolsters your success. Remember, the quality of your relationships directly impacts the quality of your life. Embrace the strategies within this chapter, and watch as your network becomes a tapestry of meaningful relationships that enrich your journey.

Chapter 10

Creating a Vision for the Future

A compelling vision is the North Star that guides your journey. In this chapter, we embark on a transformative journey to create a vision for your future—a journey that will empower you to shape your path and achieve remarkable success in the remaining part of 2023.

The Power of Vision: A clear vision acts as a compass, steering your actions and decisions toward your desired future. Understand that a strong vision is the foundation for setting meaningful goals.

Reflecting on Your Values: Your values are the core principles that define your identity. Reflect on your values and how they align with your aspirations. A vision rooted in your values is authentic and enduring.

Envisioning Your Ideal Future: Close your eyes and imagine your life a year from now. Visualize your accomplishments, your environment, and the emotions associated with your success.

Setting Long-Term Goals: Long-term goals are milestones on the path to your vision. Set ambitious goals that challenge you to grow and evolve. These goals should reflect the aspirations you've envisioned.

SMART Vision Goals: Transform your vision into actionable steps by setting SMART vision goals—Specific, Measurable, Achievable, Relevant, and Time-bound. These goals provide clarity and direction.

Creating a Vision Board: A vision board is a visual representation of your goals and aspirations. Create a board filled with images, words, and symbols that resonate with your vision. This tangible representation reinforces your commitment.

Breaking Down Vision Goals: Each vision goal can be broken down into smaller, actionable steps. These steps serve as a roadmap to your vision, guiding you towards your ultimate destination.

Daily Visualization: Spend time each day visualizing your vision. Engage your senses, immerse yourself in the emotions associated with your success, and affirm your commitment to realizing your vision.

Adaptation and Reevaluation: Your vision is not static; it evolves as you grow. Regularly reevaluate your vision and make adjustments as circumstances change. Embrace the flexibility to adapt and refine.

Perseverance and Resilience: The journey towards your vision may have challenges. Cultivate the resilience to overcome setbacks and the determination to persevere despite obstacles.

In this chapter, you're not just creating a vision; you're manifesting your future. By aligning your goals with your values and forging a path guided by your aspirations, you're steering your life toward extraordinary success. Remember, a vision is not a daydream; it's a commitment to yourself. Embrace the strategies within this chapter, and watch as your vision transforms into reality, painting a picture of achievement and fulfillment that far exceeds your expectations.

Conclusion

Your Path to Productivity and Success
Congratulations! You've embarked on a transformative journey through the chapters of this book—a journey that has equipped you with the tools, strategies, and insights to pave your path to productivity and success. As you stand at the culmination of this journey, take a moment to reflect on how far you've come and the incredible potential that lies ahead.

 Each chapter has woven a thread of transformation into the fabric of your life. From mastering time management to cultivating resilience, you've gained a repertoire of skills that are not just theoretical concepts, but practical blueprints for creating a life of purpose and accomplishment. Remember that progress isn't always monumental leaps. It's often the result of consistent, small steps forward. Embrace the journey, celebrating each victory along the way.

 Your path to productivity and success is uniquely yours. The strategies outlined in these chapters provide a framework, but it's up to you to personalize and adapt them to your circumstances and aspirations. Growth is not a destination; it's a continuous journey. Embrace the mindset of a lifelong learner, open to new possibilities, challenges, and opportunities for improvement.

 Your feedback is invaluable. As you apply these strategies and witness their impact, we encourage you to share your experiences and insights with us and fellow readers. Your stories are a source of inspiration and encouragement for others on their own journeys. If this book has resonated with you and propelled you towards positive change, we invite you to leave a review. Your words can guide others towards this transformative journey, helping them harness the power of productivity and success.

 As you close this book, a new chapter of your life begins—one shaped by intention, purpose, and the unwavering belief in your potential. Armed with the insights within these pages, you're equipped to navigate challenges, seize opportunities, and create a life that's not only productive but deeply fulfilling.

Thank you for embarking on this journey with us. Your dedication to personal growth and accomplishment is an inspiration. May your path be illuminated by the light of your aspirations, and may your journey be one of continuous achievement and boundless success.